6 STEPS TO BUILDING A STRONG FOUNDATION OF YOUR BUSINESS

Laura Little

WOW Book Publishing™

First Edition Published by Laura Little

Copyright ©2018 Laura Little

WOW Book Publishing™

ISBN: 9781729460719

All rights reserved. Neither this book, nor any parts within it may be sold or reproduced in any form without permission.

No part of this book may be reproduced in any form or by any electronic or mechanical means including information storage and retrieval systems, without permission in writing from the author. The only exception is by a reviewer, who may quote short excerpts in a review.

The purpose of this book is to educate and entertain. The views and opinions expressed in this book are that of the author based on her personal experiences and education. The author does not guarantee that anyone following the techniques, suggestions, ideas or strategies will become successful. The author shall neither be liable nor responsible for any loss or damage allegedly arising from any information or suggestion in this book.

Testimonials

"I have had the pleasure of knowing and working with Laura and am glad she is finally writing this book. If you are ready to uncover the DNA of your Business and achieve your goals, this book is for you!"

—Kirsten Welles L.
AC, RPP, CPE founding member of the Institute of Coaching at Harvard Medical School, Master Coach, Life SOULutions that Work

"I have had the pleasure of meeting Laura many years ago through our interest in golf. We have traveled the US together, plus we had the privilege of having Laura and her husband accompany my wife and I on an Alaska cruise to celebrate our 50th anniversary. I am so glad she is writing this book at this time in her life and launching her business, I know you will enjoy her book as much as we enjoy our friendship with Laura and her family."

—Melvin "Bo" Fulghum, President
AZ Companies

"Laura Little is a wealth of knowledge when it comes to running your life and business with endless vitality! She lives by her own principles and it shows! An experienced and empathic life and business vitality coach, Laura is ready to help so many business owners discover the "DNA" to better balance and growth in their lives and businesses."

—Katherine Morales, APR
President/Founder,
Inflection Point Communications, LLC

"I've known Laura for more than 10 years and have watched her use her gifts and skills to turn the 'unwinnable' into 'amazing win. She is a teacher who leads by example and this book will help you learn to apply not only what she knows but benefit from the life lessons she's learned. Champions are rarely chosen from the ranks of the "unscarred". Laura is a champion in every sense of the definition."

—Mike Jensen, President
4Atmos Technologies, LLC

"In reading Laura's book, DNA of Your Business, I was able to understand how to apply her coaching principles to my business. I believe you will find her book very helpful and practical too."

—Nan Nelson, MBA, MD

Contents

Dedication vii
Acknowledgements ix
Foreword xi

Chapter 1: Building a Strong Foundation 1
- Reaching for the Dream 3

Chapter 2: Define Your Full Spectrum Vision 9
- The Results Formula 11
- Business 13
- Philanthropy 17
- Health and Wellness 18
- Time and Money Freedom 21
- Relationships 23
- Alignment 26
- Define What You Do 30
- Understand your purpose—
  Why you do what you do 31
- How You Do it Better 33
- What Makes Your Business Special 34

Chapter 3: Connecting Vision to Cost Model 39
- Understanding Four Value Levers 42

Chapter 4: Define Your Core Strategic Model 59
- Define your Product / Service 61
- Define your Target Customer 64
- Define Your Operations and Technology 66

Chapter 5: Define Your DNA Profile 77
- Mastering Your Vision 79
- Your Unique Purpose 83
- How You Do it Better 86
- Personal Mission Statement 89
- Value Statement 90
- Your DNA Profile 92

Chapter 6: Unlocking The Code For Success 97
- Keep Going and Growing 99
- Refreshing your services and products. 102
- Refreshing, Reviewing Your Target Customers ... 105
- Refresh Your Operation and Technology 106
- Refresh Your Organization and Talent 108
- Refresh Your Finance and Accounting 110

Dedication

I wrote this book to empower sole proprietors and small business owners to rise above the conditions and situations of their daily thinking. We have been conditioned to think that working harder and longer is the only path to success. However, here is a different, better way and that is reconnecting to the DNA of Your Business to unlock the code to your success.

I dedicate this to all sole proprietors and entrepreneurs who are following their dream and hope that the words reenergize and inspire you to continue or begin to live lives of abundance and increase in alignment with your purpose.

Blessings,
Laura Little

Acknowledgements

I acknowledge the souls who are no longer here such as Glenn "Tex" Evans, Martin Luther King Jr., Nelson Mandela, Arnold Palmer, and Jane Breckenridge for their positive impacts on humanity and my life.

I am grateful for the leadership of former U. S. President Barak Obama while in office, and the models set by previous former U.S. Presidents Jimmy Carter, George H.W, Bush, Bill Clinton, and George W. Bush on how to model the life of service after holding the highest office in the land.

I acknowledge the influence and pleasure I have had from learning from being associated with people such as, but not limited to, Mary Morrissey, Kirsten Welles, John Boggs, Lou Gerstner, Ginny Rometty, Diana Sweetwood, Joe Heffernan, John Murrin, Janet Foutty, Vishal Morjaria, Les Brown, Libby Bacon, Mark Wiggins, Kevin Counihan, James Michel, Newton Wong, Josephine Sempere, Kristin Dowty, Isabelle FitzGerald, Joyce Mohr, Sally Fingar Ward, Tab Warlitner, Bo and Carolyn Fulghum, Joe Fowler, Jim Rohn, Prince EA, and Bob Proctor.

I acknowledge my family, friends, staff and the supporters of this book for their help in the process of writing and creating it.

I acknowledge my faith for guiding me in my life journey to this point.

Finally, I acknowledge you the reader, for receiving this book and using it in the most productive way you know how to evoke your vision for a successful business.

Foreword

Dear Reader,

6 Steps to Building a Strong Foundation of Your Business is the book you need to read and learn from if you are ready to discover the DNA of your business. Laura has acquired some masterful skills and experiences through her career and she has become a wealth of knowledge when it comes to running your business and coaching entrepreneurs and business owners.

This book has the power to help you find the DNA of your business in this world filled of competition and opportunity. Laura will help you to transform your thinking and guide you to make good entrepreneurial decisions. She will help you unlock the code to your success story.

Laura has the expertise, skills, spirit and knowledge necessary to help you change your mind set about business. She will guide you to discover your purpose and how it is translated into your business.

—Vishal Morjaria
International Speaker and Award-winning Author

CHAPTER 1

Building a Strong Foundation

Reaching for the Dream

> "A dream is only a dream . . . until you decide to make it real"
>
> —**Harry Styles**

You and I are living in a time of accelerating change. Over the next few years 79 million people will have joined us as entrepreneurs starting small businesses. We are living in a time when many people are recognizing the transcendental, transformational thinking of other cultures, from the Americas of one hundred years ago in Concord, Massachusetts and applying them to our lives. New entrepreneurial ventures are a manifestation of this time. Each has a unique motivation, purpose, funding model, etc. This level of competition AND opportunity for collaboration is unprecedented. This book is unique in that it takes this transformational thinking and set of principles and engages you and I in an interactive process to think through your business together.

We'll start where we as human beings start, at our DNA. What is our purpose and how does discovering that and translating that into our business help me to guide you through the process of evoking the best decisions you can make. You'll define the WHAT you do. WHY you do it. HOW you do it better. This establishes the ability to unlock the code to your success story. But we don't stop there—no, after you have a clear Vision, now you've established the roadmap to define the steps and actions you have to take to breathe life into that vision.

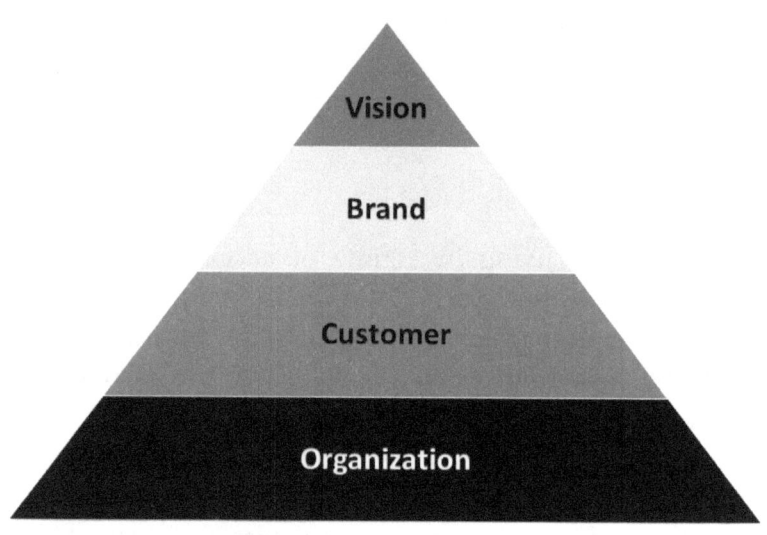

The Blueprinting process continues with defining your Brand Strategy. Then we move down the pyramid into understanding your customer and measuring the value you provide. Finally, we look at the organization. Before we launch into that process, I think its valuable to set just a bit of background information on some guiding principles that apply throughout.

You and I each have personal and or professional lives. Most business books only deal with the professional aspects of life. My approach to working with entrepreneurs is unique in that I understand that it's difficult to maintain the boundaries we like to set between them. Interwoven throughout each chapter are thought provoking questions to help you think through the personal implications of your business's strategic vision to understand the ramifications on your health and wellness, relationships and time and money freedom.

Business books often espouse the statistics on failure rates in terms of business failure, e.g. a lack of capital, marketing, sales, stagnation, etc. However, I am convinced that there is an underlying component that is the true driver, self-management and our reluctance to break through our current paradigms and thinking patterns. For startup businesses, when times are tight and families need critical items, key situations arise in the order of fact (medical crisis, extra hours, more investment vs. college savings, etc.) it's difficult to stay the course and live for your purpose, knowing that you need to model those behaviors to provide the best chance of long term success for your family.

One paradigm I see frequently is the mindset of lack or a fixed mindset versus a mindset of increase and growth. To understand the difference between a mindset of lack, and a mindset of abundance an understanding of the two Universes is critical. First there is the Physical Universe with the laws that are published by nations, states, counties, cities, etc. Many are obvious such as speed limit signs, parking signs and we understand the consequences of obeying or ignoring the laws.

In the Order of Fact, we all live in the physical universe, and will experience any number of conditions and situations every day of our lives. Some will be small. A cup of coffee is spilled and splashes all over our outfit before an important meeting. Others will be huge like the loss of a beloved family member. Second there is a Spiritual Universe, these laws are not often as well understood. Some overlap and are incorporated into our common, physical laws such as murder, theft and the other Christian Commandments. However, there are 11 spiritual laws that govern the universe and are always at work, regardless of our awareness. In the Order of Truth, we have the power to overcome circumstances and situations as the Spirit works through us or as us.

> "Until you make the unconscious conscious, it will direct your life and you will call it fate."
>
> —**C.G. Jung**

In learning to understand the Spiritual Universe and transcending or transforming the conditions we experience in Physical Universe, there are several common tenets that are often espoused by all leaders, integral or not within the new movements afoot espousing Living our Dreams and Purpose through alignment with our Spiritual purpose.

- Articulate your Vision clearly
- Attract your Vision
- Live Happily Ever After

Those leaders with integrity, add steps and examples

- *Raise Your Vibration*
- Articulate your Vision Clearly
- *Take the Steps You Can Take Every Day*
- *Set Accountability for your Actions, Live in Gratitude*
- *Set up a Spiritual Flow through Give Back and Donations*

- *Review your Results and Take the Steps you Need to Take Every Day*
- *Check in on your Vison and Live in Gratitude or Expand*

It's easy to see why anyone would struggle with the Happily Ever After approach, unless you are intrinsically gifted with already living a life of purpose and educated along those lines, it will be very difficult to attract your vision and live happily ever after without providence.

This book takes you through the process of the steps for matching the transcendent thinking with more traditional top tier consulting approaches on the steps you can take, accountabilities that can be set in place and the flow that is generated when this works together is depicted below.

"When obstacles arise, you change your direction to reach your goal; you do not change your decision to get there."

—Zig Ziglar

Notes

CHAPTER 2

Define Your Full Spectrum Vision

"I learned this, at least, by my experiment; that if one advances confidently in the direction of his dreams, and endeavors to live the life which he has imagined, he will meet with a success unexpected in common hours..."

—**Henry David Thoreau**

The Results Formula

We experience our results as small business owners in four quadrants. #1 - Health & Wellness; # 2 Business and Philanthropy; #3 Relationships; and #4 Time & Money Freedom.

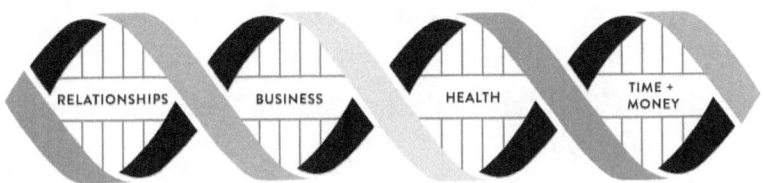

The key to success is learning this new language of success. Let's begin with the results formula and how we apply that to our business and life.

We all have results—we woke up today, looked around us and can see the results as the output of our lives. We are starting a new business as the result of a decision we made for ourselves to move to a new chapter in our professional lives. We have a certain level of health and wellness that is the direct result of the effort we have or haven't put into that quadrant. We have relationships, business, family, significant others and the quality of those relationships reflects the time and effort we put into those relationships. We also do or don't have time and money freedom.

Here is the results formula

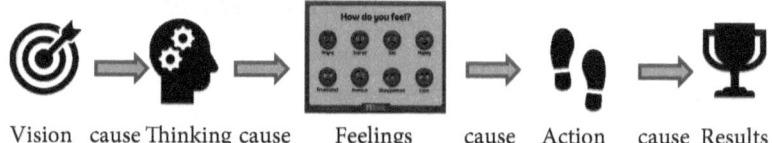

Vision   cause Thinking cause   Feelings   cause   Action   cause Results

Here are a few simple examples:

- You Think you lost your wallet, you immediately Feel panic; you race around recreating where it may be until you find it and you are immediately flooded with Feelings of relief.
- You Think about the hot date on Friday and you Feel excited.
- When you Think limiting thoughts you feel limited and when you Think expansive thoughts you feel confident.
- When you Feel limited you take different Actions that when you feel confident. Apply that to a business scenario.
- You are meeting with your customer to ask for a big sale after a fight with your best friend. Are

you able to create the separation necessary to be confident as a CEO and business owner in your business and set aside that limiting thought of the fight? Whatever Feeling you bring to the meeting will determine the energy and Actions you take in the meeting and the ultimate outcome or Result of the meeting.

Business

> "You are the master of your destiny. You can influence, direct and control your own environment. You can make your life what you want it to be."
>
> **—Napoleon Hill**

What is it that you do, what service and or product do you provide that no one else does? The answer to that question, saying it out loud reconnects you powerfully to your business. It provides the energy to the why and the purpose for the genesis of your business.

When I begin working with a business owner, they often tell me, "I've already defined my Vision for my business," and no doubt that is true for them on the level of fact. My next question is how long ago was that and what, if anything, has changed since then?

Refreshing and reviewing your vision is critical, if you are not achieving the results you want in your business. Think about sports. If you miss hit a pitch in baseball by just a bit, it's the difference between a foul ball or a home run in some cases.

In my studies with Mary Morrisey I have learned each of us has six mental faculties that come into play in developing a strong business foundation: Imagination, Perception, Will, Intuition, Reason and Memory. Developing a Vision relies largely on the faculty of the imagination; however, our brains and thought patterns or paradigms are established by age 30. To innovate, create and establish a new business means developing new paradigms and shifting into new patterns of behaviors.

Let's start with this question" Do your current services and products match up 100% to your current vision?—If not, what is the limiting factor and how can that block be removed?

Where do you see yourself one year from now—that's far enough down the road. If you look at older books and advice they will tell you to look 5 or 10 years down the road. That's too far. Technology and the pace of change is too fast. Short term is 3 months to 6 months and 1–2 years is long term nowadays.

My Business Vision

This set of exercises and the answers you provide me will tell me exactly what you do. It also reminds you of what you do. This makes it easier to take the next step in the exercise to define your Brand. We've all heard about the power of branding. Apple, McDonald, Coca Cola, etc. have that down cold. For sole proprietors, it is the WHY, the heart and soul of their business that needs to come through.

Not every entrepreneur is a born marketer, and many have just been trying to figure out how to get the message out without thinking through some key components that tell their story and unlock the code to success.

The first key component is to define how your organization creates value, go beyond the what and into your purpose for being in business. Thinking back to the answers you gave in the "what I do for services and products"—Why are you doing each of them?

Here's an example from my business.... *I have a MasterMind Coaching Level because sole proprietors often miss the experience of brainstorming and sharing ideas and success stories when they leave a corporate environment. This service offers them the opportunity to recreate that experience with likeminded business owners.*

Next is defining your core strengths. Not all of your services and products are created equal. Add a column and rank them if you are a detail-oriented entrepreneur. If not, use your intuition and rank them based on your instinctive knowledge of the value they bring your business. At this point you'll need yet another business capability memory forward thinking to determine what your future strategic drivers are. What services and products are currently big revenue producers, but may be at the end of their lifecycle? What new services and products will be needed to meet the future demands of customers in the next six months, one year and two years?

Predictive modeling and other demand services are key to understanding these needs if this isn't your area of expertise and strength. Lead time to ramp up a new operating model, technology and organization support can take time and significant funding, putting smaller businesses at a disadvantage.

Now that you are thinking about some of these deeper topics, make sure that your Vision is clearly defined. Just as the best builder in the world can't build your dream house without a set of fully approved building plans, your vision can't be reached without being clearly defined.

I recommend and use for my own business and life the principle of living from your vision and taking the actions you can take today to "reverse engineer" the process. I see the vision as already achieved then work backwards, thinking through to recreate in my mind the steps I took that helped to get to that vision. Then I take the steps I can take today, with what I have to move forward.

> "If one advances confidently in the direction of his dreams, and endeavors to live the life which he has imagined, he will meet with a success unexpected in common hours."
>
> **—Henry David Thoreau**

The universe aligns around clear decisive action and decisions to make it happen for you. When I keep moving forward each day, monitoring progress towards that vision, amazing progress falls into place.

Philanthropy

What is your vision for giving back? Is this important to you and is it something that you want to incorporate in your vision for your life? Is it something that you want to coordinate with your business vision? Does the business get credit? Or is this something entirely personal? Is this part of your personal vision where giving back is something related to tithing to your church, synagogue, or other religious entity? Is this something you do anonymously and don't want any credit for. Or is it something that you do as a business and you do in part because you believe in it and in part because it's related to the business that you own and part of the purpose in the reason why you did it. An example of tying a philanthropic venture to a business may be , if you are a person who values children and has a business related to children, then do something related to, for example, the boys and girls clubs or the girl scouts, boy scouts, something related to a children's group as their give back of choice, So that retains that connection to children and it's something meaningful to their new business and their identity to who they were and provides that continuity.

My Philanthropy Vision

Think through how you want to retain that continuity, if at all, and what that vision looks like, how do you incorporate that? Or into your life, into your business vision, and into your life vision, how do you make that work seamlessly with both your life and work balance? Because that's really why I'm having you do this exercise, for the vision of your life because we'll get to how you align the work vision and the life and business visions in the next step. If your give back is aligned to your business, then does that create market opportunities for discounts, other opportunities to engage your customers to help support that philanthropy and to create new ideas that can give you life, support your vision, support your business and enable it to grow and empower you in both your business vision and your life vision? In that way, it can be an energizing and empowering part of doing this exercise.

Health and Wellness

After you've defined the vision for your business, for sole proprietors, small business owners, something that's often overlooked is defining the vision for your life. The Individual is the Business to a large extent. Keeping health and wellness at the forefront is especially important for small businesses and sole proprietors. If you're lying in a bed sick, you are not earning revenue, unless you have developed a passive revenue generating business model. ***It is just that simple.***

Taking care of your health and wellness is not typically part of the business plan for many sole proprietors. I don't know why, but I see it over and over and over and over again in my clients. They say, "I'm the breadwinner, I'm the money earner, and I have to go out. I don't care if I have a stomachache, I don't care if I have a cold or this or that ailment. I have to go and it doesn't matter if I'm under the weather. "I'm going to go work, and I'm going to go and provide before I take care of my health."

And then what happens? Their health declines, their energy levels go down, their productivity goes down, and what happens to the business's results? They go down too. Your hairdresser shows up ill, they've got a cold, they got germs, who wants to sit in that chair? You're a small business owner, and customers are sneezing and coughing all over you. Do you want to stay at that store and touch the money that they have touched? Be coughed on while they wait on you? No! You may get that sale that day, but are they going to come back? No. Okay, maybe you can make a case for an online business and sitting behind a computer and it's easier. But, are you going to feel up to giving the same level of customer service? And are you going to have that energy and that attitude and all of those things to bring to the table?

We've explored the some of the consequences for low energy, health and wellness. Let's explore your vision for Health and Wellness. What are you doing every day to show up with that high energy, that high vibration, and to protect your immunity? How are you working in exercise, fitness, nutrition, and good eating habits into your life to protect and sustain the business that's the lifeblood of your family and your income? Those are other things that are often overlooked by small business owners because they look at them as lost time, personal distractions. However, coming into work each morning refreshed, knowing that you have put time on your calendar for a work out, planned for dinner with family or friends, made time to go to the grocery store and have healthy habits in control means those things aren't in the back of your mind taking up extra cycles. Write it down, what do your health and your wellness mean to you and the vision for caring for yourself first and then having predictable energy for your business?

My Health and Wellness Vision

Think about the last time you took a trip on an airplane. They tell you to put on your own oxygen mask first before you help someone else with theirs. At first, it may seem counterintuitive, but you have to take care of yourself. Because if your oxygen is depleted you can't help anyone else with their mask if you're passed out. However, if you put your oxygen on first, then you can help someone else. Take care of your health first, then you can take care of your business and be the best that you can be and make the business culture that you want it to be.

Time and Money Freedom

Time and Money Freedom is the next dimension I want you to think about. Many sole proprietors and small business owners reach a certain level of success and one of the key parts of my platinum program is work-life balance because they realize they're working 60, 80, 100 hours per week. They've reached a level of monetary freedom or business success; however, they don't necessarily have time freedom. They need to redefine the work-life balance differently in their life. Others are just starting out, and maybe they have time freedom but they don't have any money freedom yet, and they're just in the launch phase. So how do we plan for time and money freedom? Think through where you're at now, and what your personal ideal balance is. Do you love to work? Or are you a person who wants more time freedom? Maybe that varies by the point you're at in your life. Maybe it was perfect when you started your business and now you're meeting me or another business vitality coach, or you're just getting this book because you're looking for possibilities to redefine where you're at in your life because you're searching for new answers and new possibilities.

This is the thing to think about here, define what you would love. Define your ideal work day and go from there. How does it start? What time of day does it start? How long do you take at home before you start your work day? Then what's your ideal work day? Look at your calendar. Use your calendar as a scheduling tool to black out the things that are important to you and not as a weapon. So many people are driven by their calendars and feel like they are slaves to their calendar. How can you reframe that so that you own your calendar? The way to achieve time and money freedom is to have a forward view of your calendar. Take a hold of your calendar in advance. You're looking at the calendar on your day off, or ahead of time and choosing what you are going to do?

My Time and Money Freedom Vision

In order to make a change, or a choice for your vision, you will start with these fundamental three choices. What can I stop doing myself? What do I continue doing? What do I start doing? How do I assign value and black out that time? Where do I place the things that are most important to me in advance? Then, let the calendar fill up with the other things, so that I make sure that I have prioritized whatever it is that's the most important to me. Is it my business? What parts of my business are the most important to me, give me life, and that I personally am going to do? What things am I going to delegate to someone else? Am I going to hire someone, contract someone to do this or that?

Think back to Chapter One and the discussion on understanding the "What you do," "Why you do it" and "How you do it better." This will ground you as you make those critical choices in Stopping, Continuing or Starting activities, prioritizing them so that you maximize your time efficiently. Now you can focus on the what, and the why that I defined in the previous activities that we just talked through and we just looked at. Go back to the roots of your purpose and why you started this business and that's what you focus on. Your core DNA, and that's what gives you a healthy business and locks your energy and your focus on what's driving your results. And then you hand off and delegate those activities that need to be done for any business. But you find somebody else that wants to do that and those activities give them life and you give them the opportunity to earn a living doing those things that give them life. And that's how your business thrives and prospers.

Relationships

In order to have a healthy, long-lasting, thriving business you need to have healthy relationships. You need to make time for relationships, whether they're family relationships, a significant other, all kinds of different relationships in your life. Therefore, you need to define the vision for the kinds of relationships that you want to cultivate and maintain in your life. Does your family live in the same area as you do? What amount of time do you want to allocate in your life to spending with the family that you have in your area? And how does the business and the hours that you spend with your business interrelate to that?

Part of crafting this vision for our life is relationships. We all have relationships and we need a clear vision for all of our relationships looking at all different levels: extended family, friends, and significant others. Think through what, going back to what I mentioned earlier, an ideal day looks like. How do you balance work and life from a relationship perspective? We talked about it from a time perspective before. But what does it look like from a relationship perspective? Who are you spending your time with? How do you make time for the people that you care about? Is it virtual? Is it face to face? And how do you make sure that you have, yeah, the cliché "quality time" with those people that you value? I know I have spent so much time with people over the years traveling. And all of us found creative ways to spend time remotely, through FaceTime, Skype, phone calls, whatever it was, staying engaged with our families while we were traveling and on the road. Some more successfully than others.

Some of us made a whole repertoire of friends that live all around the country. And maintaining those friendships is a challenge. Right? Many of you are in the same situation. With a very mobile society, we might have friends and family who don't even live in the same country. How do we maintain this complex set of family and friendships on a virtual, global and local scale, and make it work for us? And

Define Your Full Spectrum Vision

still run a successful, profitable business? It takes thought, it takes planning, and no, it's not romantic always, it's not glamorous, but it is important. So think through what that look like, and works like and have those conversations with the people that are important to you. Are weekends to be declared work-free zones or can you scaffold between business and relationship activities to balance everything out between all the demands based on each of those different relationships. Work through the calendar, figure all that out, write it down, figure out what that vision looks like and think it through. But the main thing is, write it down.

Take some time to think about the vision for each of those relationships and take the time to create the vision for each of those relationships. As you go through this exercise, keep in mind social relationships, business networking, your extended relationships, etc. Another key concept is that each one will have a different value, a different time dimension, different drivers, and a different time allocation based on the different goals you have in mind. Being intentional doesn't undermine, it enhances the relationships that you want to cultivate.

My Relationship Vision

Make time, make that a clear vision, document that vision, what does it look like? Articulate it, write it down, have it in mind, and really thinking it through in a purposeful, intentional manner really sets the tone and the priority for that and, like any new kind of thought process, make sure that you then revisit that vision—if this is a new thing to you—fairly frequently after you've first done this. Nurture it, keep it in mind, keep it fresh in mind and keep it relevant, keep it vital, if this is a new process for you to establish a habit of making sure that you make time for relationships as you work that into your business model, and making time for that, and making sure that relationships become a valued part of your life and your business, and making time for that is important. Keep it at hand, because you're going to need it for the next exercise as we turn to the next part of the book.

Alignment

You have accomplished two big things at this point. We have designed at your business vision and your life vision. Now we create alignment between those two visions. Let's look at the opportunities and challenges between the business and life visions. What we want to do is compare the business vision and the life vision and see where we find the greatest amount of alignment and fit. Are you a person who has grandiose dreams in every aspect of your life? Do you want the biggest and best business, the biggest and best life, the biggest and best relationships, foundations, charities, and the biggest and best of everything? That's fantastic. I can support that. But sometimes there are tradeoffs you need

Define Your Full Spectrum Vision

if you're going to have all those things, then the ability to have strong funding, strong finances and other things in place, and a strong strategy to make those happen as well as the discipline and prioritization to make those tradeoffs, prioritization, at the right time, right place to make all of that work together, fit together, and make the right decisions that are going to make that happen. So you'll need a couple of tools.

We've mentioned the calendar several times, to make that calendar work for you as a structure and a guidebook for how you calendar all of those things that are your priorities and make the time and schedule your priorities first and then fill in with the things that are less of a priority. There's a great story that I heard once and it goes like this; If you're trying to fit a series of ping pong balls, pebbles, and sand and water into the same jar, if you fill the jar with the sand first, then you'll never have room for the ping pong balls or the pebbles. If you fill your day answering emails, small complaints, the trivial or the sand as in this analogy, you'll never have the big priorities, the big gains, or dreams, or goals. But if you fill your calendar, your life, with the ping pong balls first, then you put in the pebbles, or the next tier of priorities, or things that are going to get you to where you need to go. Then you let the grains of sand fill in the available spaces, then put the water in, there's room for some of everything. So keep that analogy and those things in mind as you're filling out your calendar.

Start with the big things, start with the top priorities and don't get overwhelmed, If you've got fifty things on your calendar and they appear in some random order, then first thing you do with your cup of coffee, cup of tea, Red Bull, or beverage of your choice in the morning that gets you started, then go through them and prioritize and of the fifty, if you start with number one, and you work on that until it's complete, and then you go to number two, and you go to number three, even if you don't knock all fifty things off in the day, you can satisfy yourself that at the end of the day, you worked on what was most important and put your time in the right place instead of being distracted by circumstances, or situations.

Calendar for the month of _____

Sunday	Monday	Tuesday	Wednesday	Thursday	Friday	Saturday

Yes, something critical may arise during the course of the day, and you may have to take a break, reprioritize. That's the way life is. But during the reprioritization, there may be something else that comes up, that's urgent, but is it more important? And that activity of reprioritizing will you help you to decide if it's just merely urgent or if it's more important than those things already on the list. Does it go in the jar first or does it go in the jar later in the day? You figure out where it fits on your calendar and you manage your calendar, instead of letting your calendar manage you.

Continuing in that same vein, another tool is a gratitude journal. For areas of alignment, where you're in complete alignment between your business vision and your life vision, I recommend creating a gratitude journal. That way, throughout the day, at the end of the day, first thing in the morning, whatever kind of person you are, morning person, evening person, or just somebody who needs a pick me up during the middle of the day for assisting in energy on a bad day, you've got something that really reinforces what you're doing and that you are on track. Your business and your life are working in harmony together and continuing to look at that and each area where your business and life are working in harmony, helps those days where it gets out of whack, where the kids are sick, or something else happens, the car breaks down, circumstances, situations, life intervenes, and things get all out of sync and things just don't go according to plan.

We all have those days where we are tempted to think "Oh my gosh, this is a permanent situation." But, when you have that grounding and that point of reference, it's easy to pull yourself back in and say "No, this is the exception and this where am I as a whole. My business is in alignment, my life is in alignment and this is the exception, I can weather the exception." And then, that gives you that grounding to say "All right". Then, if you see a pattern, and this is happening more and more frequently, then you can ask "How does this affect my strategic decisions?" Maybe there is something that's happening pretty frequently in my business and there are disruptions. Now, do I need to take a look at my strategic direction? Is something happening pretty frequently in my business, on a day-to-day basis and it's being disrupted?" If this is happening on a repeated basis, this can be a revelatory experience for you to say, "Hmm, there's something to this, this is no longer a set of exceptions, this is now becoming a pattern, this is becoming a trend."

Now you can get in front of this and you can make a new strategic decision and say:—this is what I need to get in front of, this is what I need to look at and a new decision that I need to make about the direction of where I need to head to now; to make a better decision and off this, plan and do it intentionally, strategically, and put all of the things in place to become more successful. That's where you find your power and plan for the future.

Define What You Do

The objective of this book is to establish a strong foundation for a new business. It may seem simplistic, however, being able to state in a single sentence what you do is hard for some entrepreneurs and small business people. Even most elevator speeches are 2 to 3 sentences. Take some time and write out your sentence. If it's too difficult to capture the essence of what you do in a single sentence, then select no more than three bullet points on what you do.

What is your product or service offering?

Product or Service—What Do I Do?

You will need to use this in multiple documents and for multiple purposes:

- Business Plan
- Marketing Plan
- Social Media Messaging
- Elevator Speeches and Magnetic messaging

Other elements to consider here as you create the documents above are the facts about how you deliver your products/services (e.g. brick and mortar, online, both, specialized expertise, etc.)

Understand your purpose—Why you do what you do

There are many purposes for starting your own business.

- Are you a true entrepreneur? Do you have a burning desire to be your own boss, and build a venture?

- Are you a person who was laid off and looking to replace your income as a contractor in your current field?

- Are you a person who went down a practical degree and career path and now has the money freedom to pursue a vocation you've always wanted to pursue?

- Are you a person who is setting up a business to create an environment and culture? For example: a café because you love social interaction in your community?

Purpose/Passion– Why I Do What I Do?

Understanding why you do what you do can make the difference between success and failure. Are you surprised? Did you think that funding was the reason that 4 of 5 small businesses failed? No, it is a contributing cause, but not the root cause.

The reason most small businesses fail is that most businesses are started by someone with technical skills—a great chef, baker, salesperson, IT person or other person with great technical skills in their area of expertise.

Define Your Full Spectrum Vision

The Fatal Assumption is—"if you understand the technical work of a business, you understand a business that does technical work"—Michael E. Gerber.

The Why is the burning desire, the deep motivation that carries you through the circumstances, situations and challenges you will face. It gives you the motivation to learn, to grow to ask for help, to network and discover what makes you special and how you do it differently. To tell yourself and your target audience (clients, bankers, venture partners, trading partners, suppliers, etc.) your compelling story with clarity and power.

How You Do it Better

At this point, you may be combining the what and why—I have developed a different point of view, theory or attitude from my industry/profession that sets me apart in this way. The key is to emphasize your unique gifts, talents, etc. NOT to strike out at a potential competitor. This is your story about what value your target clients will get from working with or buying from you.

Point of View/Philosophy

Along these lines, you likely have a point of view and are keenly aware of what your target client's biggest problem or opportunity is today.

#1 Problem/Opportunity

Note also any exceptional features your product has that addresses the problem or unique skillset you have in addressing the opportunity above.

What Makes Your Business Special

In working with Katherine Morales, I learned one of her key brand story differentiators was to be intentional in articulating "What Makes Your Business Special " when defining your brand story. If you have already defined your company's values, this next exercise will be completed more quickly than if you haven't already completed that part of your start up activities. Understanding how your company's values directly connect to delivery of your product and services is essential. Your next exercise is to create your customer value statement.

Customer Value Statement—What matters most is that my customers feel _____ and know _____.

Next, we flip perspectives and look at ourselves through the lens of our prospective customers. If, as a start up, you are fortunate to have immediate customers, ask them directly, rather than completing this exercise as a theoretical exercise. If not, then complete the exercise and then continue to validate your assumptions by taking the pulse of customers as you move from startup into the next growth phase of your business.

My Customer Values These Products/Services

Now, when you add what you want to be known for, you will have built the compelling story of your business. This is where most business coaches stop. Understanding that the individual is the business, it is important to understanding your unique code for success, your personality type.

> "Just as you car runs more smoothly and requires less energy to run faster and farther when the wheels are in perfect alignment, you perform better when your thoughts, feelings, emotions, goals and values and in balance."
>
> **—Brian Tracy**

Notes

CHAPTER 3

Connecting Vision to Cost Model

> "The greatest thing in this world is not so much where we stand as in what direction we are moving."
> —**Johann Wolfgang von Goethe**

Before you and I think about cost models and review your business and life Vision statements, it is important to keep in the front of your mind your vision for your revenue targets, your desired time investment, what level of customer experience you want to create and how each of your services and products contribute to that customer experience. If you haven't fleshed out all of those aspects of the vision, we'll work through that in the discussion topics that follow. It may take you longer to read through each topic as you may take notes, stop and think through how the examples I give apply to your business and may even stop and come back after doing some work.

Don't take too long! The business world keeps moving!

Thinking about your life vision is also valuable. We'll be discussion balancing acts; key tradeoffs and you'll need to make some key decisions to move the energy forward in your business.

> "You have brains in your head.
> You have feet in your shoes.
> You can steer yourself any direction you choose."
> —**Dr. Seuss, Oh, The Places You'll Go!**

Now that you have reviewed your vision. The next step in preparing for a coaching session or to do this on your own, using the book as your guide, is to assemble all of your relevant documentation. Key documents you'll want to have at hand depend on where you are at in your business lifecycle. Look at the table and see where you are at and the types of documents that are usually most helpful.

Start Up	Accelerator	Work Life Balance	Transition
Start Up Loan	Recent Balance Sheet Statements	Accelerator Document List	Accelerator Document List
Business Plan	Recent Profit/Loss Statements	Personal and Work Calendars	Training and Process Documentation
Marketing Plan	Recent Competitive Analysis	Job Descriptions	Job Descriptions
	Current Operating Reports		
	Technology		

Understanding Four Value Levers

This is a concept that I worked with as part of business, organization transformation and strategy practices at top consulting firms, such as Deloitte. When we are coming from the vision we need to source the actions needed to bridge from the current state, which for most readers will be brand new start up, to a going concern producing revenue. Now we're into defining your business costs and driving value is done by four primary levers. Let's look at the value and some key definitions before we get into the meat of this. Delivering value to the business is important to strategic tradeoffs. And taken together, they can drive the vision that you've just put together and the design of your organization. The four levers work in pairs.

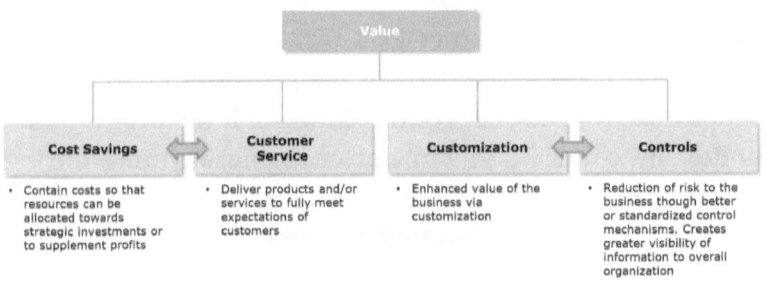

In the first pair of value levers Cost Savings versus Customer Service. Often cost savings and customer service are two tradeoffs that work together. One option is to you can look at contain costs, so that resources can be allocated toward strategic investments, or to supplement profits. Another perspective is to feature customer service to deliver products and services to fully meet the expectations of your customers. Any position in between is where you can land on the value spectrum.

There is another pair of value levers. Customization versus Controls. Customizations allow you to enhance the value of your business through customization. I offer exactly what my customers are expecting. I make one-off products or services that are designed to fit the customer's exact specifications.

I make designer pursers, designer shoes, designer whatever to the customer's specifications. What I build for customer x versus customer y is always different. Then there are Controls. The reduction of risk to my business through better standardization and control mechanisms creates greater visibility and information to tell me how I can control the organization and my manufacturing process. I make one set of products and they go to every single customer, which means that I can possibly make the best purse out there. But every single customer gets that same purse, or those same shoe, because I've refined the process and everything is optimized within my control to make it the best product under my control and I'm not changing anything during that process to vary it for customer x or customer y. This is the Ford Model T process to the extreme.

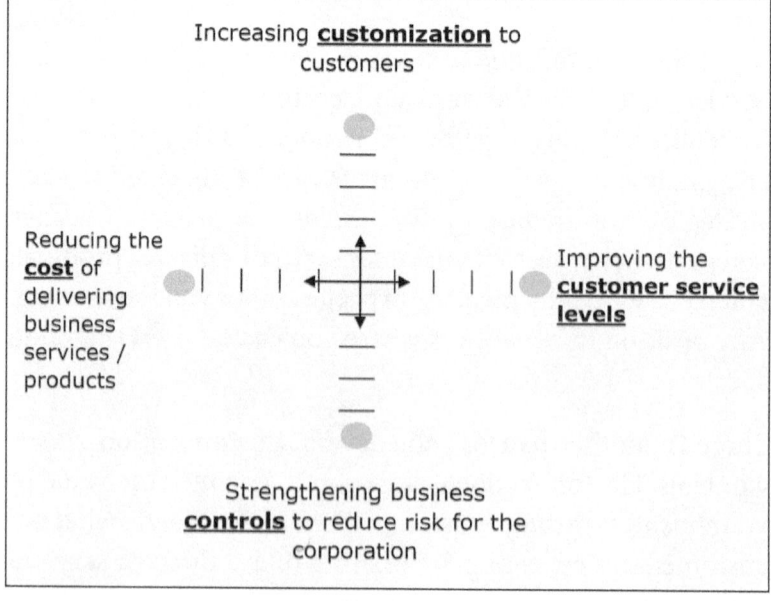

Connecting Vision to Cost Model 45

Similarly, we can see where there's a tradeoff then between Customizations and Controls, you need to decide if, as a business owner, where you're going to place the balance and the tradeoffs between those various levers in order to respect your funding model, your cost structure, customer service, and the level of product customizations and process controls that you want to offer to make it make sense for the vision that you want to offer your customers.

As you determine your value drivers, you bring into play one of our six mental faculties, perception. You can choose how you see each circumstance and situation from your perspective as a business owner and from the perspective of your target customer. It will be ideal to do each of these exercises first as the business owner and then go back and review it from the perspective of the target customer. If time doesn't permit, then definitely focus on your perspective as the target business owner. Keep in mind that you do have a specific target audience as your customer while you're making some of these key decisions and tradeoffs for your value drivers.

It will also be important to take into perspective: do you have a growth mind set or a fixed mind set? Here's an example of that: one entrepreneur may have the exact same budget as another. Say that budget is $50,000 to launch their business. The first entrepreneur sees nothing but opportunities to serve and grow. But the other may be so focused on their perception that their startup funds are too limited or too small to get going and they see the hurdles that are in front of them, and all the costs that are mounting with each and every decision. While, I never recommend going into debt to the point that you can't recover, a growth mindset, in my experience, tends to yield a better outcome, rather than focusing on what your limitations and constraints are. It helps you make better long-term decisions for the health of your business. Start with what you have, because you always have more than you realize. The graphic in the book here illustrates the main decisions that you're going to have to focus on in balancing out the value drivers. First, on the horizontal axis is cost savings and customer service. Containing costs so that resources can be allocated towards strategic investments, to supplement profits versus customer service, delivering products and/or services to fully meet expectations of customers.

Somewhere on that horizontal axis is where you're going to have to figure out where you want to land. And then also customization versus controls, making everything one-off or controls on replicating things over and over again to have standardization to control mechanisms and have repeatability. So those are the value levers that every business owner has to go through and look at to think through where they want to land on these value driver scales. Each business person has to decide that for themselves and every single consulting company and coach on the planet has a methodology for how they want to do that, and there are standard prescriptions and hypothesis that many will come in and say "You should do it this way, you should do it this way." However, I believe that your vision should be your guide. Yes, you can ask your coach "What has worked for other businesses? What do some of my competitors do?" to get a reality check and understand what the marketplace might bear and help you to get information, always do your due diligence. However, in the end, it comes down to what you are most comfortable with. You have to wear multiple hats as a small business owner. Chairman of the Board, CEO, Manager, Technician, until you delegate or contract those roles to other people.

That's always important. however, your vision for your business is what differentiates you, what makes it your signature business, and gets you back to the why, and it's also important to how your business fits into your life vision. What are the tradeoffs? If you want to have more time at home with your family, you may increase your cost in order to bring in more money and delegate some tasks in order to be able to not spend 100 hours a week at your business and still offer a good level of customer service. You may cut back on customization so that you're not spending as much time making everything a one-off and put in some controls or some standardization, so you have some things that are repeatable and predictable, so that you can go home on a regular basis and there again, you're not spending extra hours every day building in that customization and that extra level of detail and enhancements to every single order so that you can spend that time with your family. Those are the decisions that you make. Somebody else who really values those other things may make a different decision. And that's why it's really important that you understand the why of why it makes you different and your purpose for being in business and how your business fits into your life vision as you make these critical decisions.

As you may have gathered, a lot of this is a balancing act as you look at these value drivers. And another of the six mental faculties that comes into play is will. And I'm not talking about will power, we've all heard a lot about that when it comes to diets, or other aspects of things that are push energy. Now I'm talking about will in the aspect of what will cause us to create pull energy. What are the things that are so important, that drive us to create the kind of energy that pulls us to do it, that makes it easy to spend the day doing what we want to do? What are those wildly important goals that we have for our business and that also are wildly important goals for our relationship, our health, and for our time and money freedom. Those are the things you have to keep in the forefront as you create this balancing act. Statistics show that if you have more than two to three wildly important goals at any one point, you won't achieve your desired effect. Bottom line choose two wildly important goals and focus on those.

What are those wildly important goals? Pick maybe one for your business and one from another aspect of your life and think them through very carefully. Then what you need to do is to make sure that they are measurable. So maybe if I'm in the stage where I have a business and I want to accelerate my growth, maybe I'm at the point where I want to attract five thousand new target clients. So that's a clearly stated objective goal that's measurable. The next step is to determine what is my current result. For example, it may be one thousand. then, I set what my desired result at five thousand. The next question is by when? We'll set it at a year from today.

Take a step back now and do some analysis. Is it achievable? Is it realistic? To objectively analyze that some questions you may ask are: How long did it take me to get to that thousand customers? Have I been in business just three months? So maybe five thousand is realistic. Or have I been in business for fifteen years and it's taken me that long to get to a thousand.

Wildly Important Goal(s)

After the analysis, the next step is to put in place actions that can help you achieve those goals. Introspection about your capabilities, strengths are good here:

- I am comfortable looking for new customers.
- I have the tools and support in place to reach those goals.
- I have earned this income level before and am comfortable at that level.
- What new strategies am I truly able to employ that would make that result realistic?
- Thinking about strategic planning, what is something that I am going to decide to do?
- Are there things that I need to continue to do to maintain the whirlwind of my business?
- And what are some things that I could stop doing?

Stop Doing Myself	Continue Doing	Start Doing

It is important to understand that the activities in the Stop list can be both Stop altogether (unproductive activities that don't contribute to any aspect of your business or life vision) and tasks that could be delegated and/or done by somebody else because they need to continue to be done by the business, just not necessarily by me. The continue to do tasks are the activities that are true needle movers that move you forward in your business or life. Finally, what are some things I need to start doing in order to achieve that goal on top of what I'm already doing? This table documents how I am going to reallocate my time.

The operating premise is that I have been spending a hundred percent of my time doing what I'm doing today. Now am I making a decision to reduce that constant whirlwind of activities down to eighty percent of my activity load. This frees up 20% of my time to reallocate to focus on this new, wildly important goal. Then, as with any new habit or change, we employ the self-leadership and discipline to make sure that I focus that newly freed up time on the right activities to make sure that I balance that time out correctly and get the desired results to move and accelerate my results.

Let's recap here.

- Consider the possibilities
- Stay focused on ideas that are going to drive your wildly important goals.
- Rank, if you've got more than one wildly important goal, rank those by impact to narrow it down to two to three so that you can focus and maybe implement them in stages, so that you make sure you focus and get the results that you want.
  - Test the top ideas, are those ideas predictive?
  - Are they influenceable by you?
  - Can you really make sure that you do this?
- Condense your whirlwind down to 80% of my time.
  - Stop doing some of things you're doing today.
  - Continue the needle moving activities.
  - Start new activities tied to the wildly important goal.
- Free up 20% of your time.
  - Determine how you will measure the activity.
  - How are you going to measure progress towards the goal.

6 Steps to Building a Strong Foundation

In this chapter, this is more illustrative, and first we opened with the diagram that showed the horizontal and vertical axis plotted out to show some footprint designs of how these value drivers can be plotted out between cost and customer service on the horizontal axis, and customization and controls on the vertical axis. So you start with that as a blank because every business needs to design this for themselves. Then, we'll walk through just briefly some common footprints that can show you how your business might plot out as you make decisions in different ways. So if you were going to go for a cost efficient model, it may look like the first, where you're balanced between customization and controls on the vertical axis, and you're very conscious and skewed towards cost savings on the left side. And it's not very high on the customer service side on that plot. So that's how this would plot out if you're looking at a very cost-efficient model. You're finding a balance between customization and controls and you're looking at opportunities at every turn to drive cost savings into your business to look to buy in bulk, to look for quantity discounts, to look for repeatability, and to maybe do things, take on things yourself as often as possible to limit exposure and overhead and turn that around and keep facilities low, overhead low, and all kinds of those kinds of things in low order, keep your inventory low, your supply chain cost low, and turn things around just in time to make sure that your cost savings are in check. That's what that kind of a model would represent.

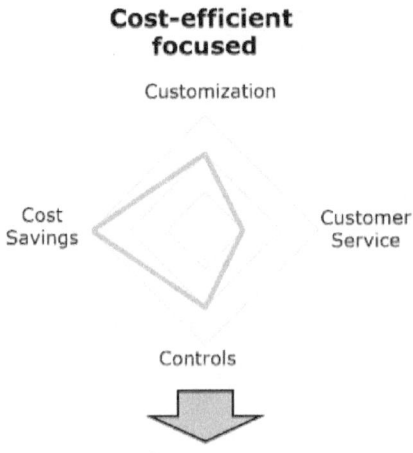

The second model represents a value-based model. There again, your cost savings are over to the left hand side, but you're looking at high customization. You're really working with your customer hand-in-hand to see exactly what they want. This often is seen in a service-based business as opposed to a product-based business where you don't have to have a lot of inventory, supplies, and stock on hand, where you don't have to productize everything and build actual products to order but you can do services to order.

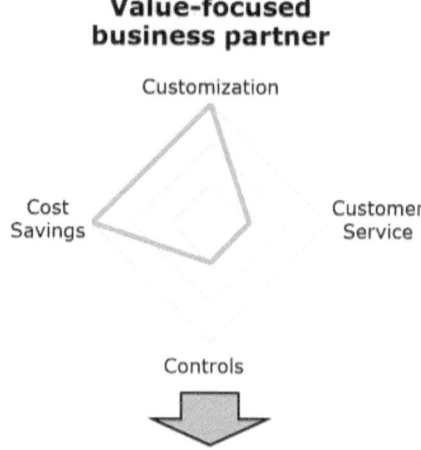

This can also be done in a coaching or a consulting business. A hair stylist can very easily take on this model where they can work with each individual customer and find exactly what kind of hairstyle each customer wants, because their costs are the same regardless of what hairstyles they perform for that customer, correct? It's those kinds of businesses that can work very efficiently with this kind of a model where they can keep a level product base and still perform very tailored services to what their customer needs and help give them exactly what they want and provide that kind of an experience.

A high touch model is where you provide high customization, high customer service at the expense of cost savings so this would be where you have very low inventory and maybe you are an online business and your customer places a very highly customized order online and you don't have a catalogue with an inventory on hand and you make each order to suit that particular customer's desires and then you put in the appropriate lead time, commensurate with that time it takes to build that customer order. This works often in a high-end furniture business. They maybe don't have any stock on hand or any models—everything is built exactly to order. You work with an interior designer and they build a particular piece of furniture exactly to fit that particular space in that particular home and as a result, then, the price and the lead time it takes to build that particular piece is longer than going to a store and buying a similar sofa, but it is made to order for that customer's space.

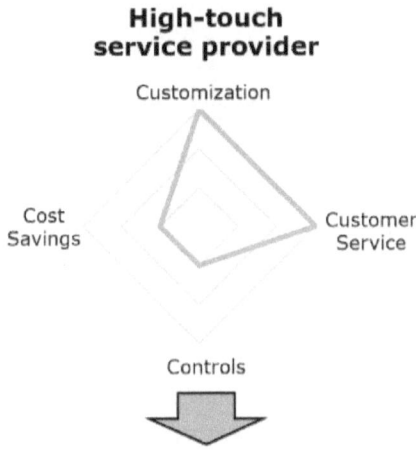

In a compliance and control-focused model, as you see this in the graphic, it's skewed in a completely different way. It's all about the controls and everything is there. You see this often in highly regulated industries such as pharmaceuticals and things that are very highly regulated and the quality must be there and it must attain certain standards before the product can be released to the public. So all of those things, every step, must be highly regulated. Other industries might be water purification, food industries, various sort of things have to meet certain standards. Therefore, they are highly regulated and controlled before things can go out to the public and make sure that the safety and every aspect of those things are respected and put into place. So those are the kinds of things. So it fits the type of business, the type of industry that you're in as well as your vision and those kinds of things. So these are the kinds of models and things that you're going to want to keep in mind as you're going through and thinking through those decisions you need to make.

Compliance & control focus

Customization

Cost Savings

Customer Service

Controls

"I've learned that fear limits you and your vision. It serves as blinders to what may be just a few steps down the road for you. The journey is valuable, but believing in your talents, your abilities, and your self-worth can empower you to walk down an even brighter path. Transforming fear into freedom—how great is that?"
—**Soledad O'Brien**

Notes

CHAPTER 4

Define Your Core Strategic Model

"There is a vitality, a life force, an energy, a quickening that is translated through you into action, and because there is only one of you in all of time, this expression is unique. And if you block it, it will never exist through any other medium and it will be lost. The world will not have it. It is not your business to determine how good it is nor how valuable nor how it compares with other expressions. It is your business to keep it yours clearly and directly, to keep the channel open. You do not even have to believe in yourself or your work. You have to keep yourself open and aware to the urges that motivate you. Keep the channel open.... No artist is pleased. [There is] no satisfaction whatever at any time. There is only a queer divine dissatisfaction, a blessed unrest that keeps us marching and makes us more alive than the others."

—**Martha Graham**

Define your Product / Service

We're going to take a look at defining your core strategic model. So first up, we're going to look at defining your services and or products. So that's the first question. Are you doing products, services, or both? Let's look at products first. Are you doing core tangible products at all? Also, assume for the purposes of this that you are. So how many products are you going to offer? In the case of a person who is going into for instance, the leather goods business, how many products are you going to offer? Let's say we start with purses. How many styles are you going to offer? Are they going to be small, or big satchels? And then are you going beyond that? Are you going into wallets? Are you going beyond ladies? Are you going into men's? Are you going into briefcases? Are you going into other types of leather accessories? Are you going into belts, iPod cases, iPad cases, other kinds of travel accessories, maybe men's cases for travel for to go inside the luggage?

Product / Service Definition

There are all kinds of different possibilities to do a whole suite of things. What does your vision tell you? Where is the cut off line? Prioritization and sequencing may be the keys based on your bandwidth. Where are you starting and what things are for future phases? So those are the decisions that you need to look at and once you've made that decision, when is that product line stable, predictable, and regularly priced? When are you going to have a steady stream of standard products that you're offering at a regular price and when

Define Your Core Strategic Model

is that going to happen on a regular basis? Now you know that suite of offerings, do you need a catalogue? Are there that many different shapes, colors, sizes, price lines, different types of leather? Are you sticking with regular cow's leather or going into different models? Are some going to be vinyl or nylon to go beyond leather, to go for PETA or other people who have objections to leather? What does this all look like? And then, what production and or wholesale sources are available to make sure that your continuity and everything is in place form a supply chain perspective. And we will delve more into supply chain as a whole as a whole another bullet point. Looking at that, from that one small example of a leather goods supply, you can see that this could get pretty complex and there are many decisions and actions you can take.

You need to think this through and to find, very carefully, what your vision is, and then all of the relative decisions that need to be made alongside of that, document them into a business plan of action. Then, moving into services, what are the support services that you need to support this product line? Obviously, there are going to be returns at some point. Not one hundred percent of everyone is going to be happy. How are they going to come back? Are they going to be come back through mail order? Are they coming back to brick and mortar? How are things going to be reprocessed, re-shelved, all of those things need to be put into place as well as the services around them. Are there staff going to be dedicated to just that? Or are the same people that are going to be handling new sales and new services also going to be handing that?

Define your Target Customer

Decisions bring clarity and the next thing in your strategic model that you need to define is your target customer. Now that you have your product and or service defined, who is most likely going to want that product and or service? In the case of the leather goods, who is your ideal customer? How do they want to interact with you? Why do they want your leather goods as opposed to other leather goods products that are already out on the market? What sets your products apart? What is going to be different about what you are bringing to the table? What sets that apart? That is what you need to be thinking about very clearly and being able to articulate in your vision so that you can very clearly communicate that to your target customer. Thinking through that, how frequently will they want to hear from you? What are they going to want to know? In many studies regarding how we interact with our customers in modern times, it's very important to give before you ask for something. The formula is give seven times before you ask! What is it that we could be giving?

Target Customer Definition

Here are examples: discuss what's new in the industry. Discuss what's new about how leather goods are made. Lead the discussion on changing trends. Provide your thoughts on the safety of the products or how the dyes that are being used or not being used at all. Discuss the process or pull back the curtain on how the product is being made. Discuss your differentiators that will resonate with your target audience or will make it more appealing. Look for opportunities to give back in terms of knowledge and things that create an audience, a demand for people who are going to want to buy your product. What are those things that you can put out on social media and other areas, YouTube videos that you can create, interests you can draw to make yourself an authority figure and not just another voice in the clutter and whirlwind that is the constant media that is out there and set yourself apart.

Then return to your brand strategy opportunities and what's in it for them? Is it quality? Is it convenience? Is it price? Is your product going to be custom? Is it more consistent? Is it more durable? What is it about your product that's going to resonate with them? And then, you ask them to buy, right? And how long is their decision time? Is this an impulse buy for them? Do they want to think it over? Do they research it? Where do you need to be? Are you going to be competing with Coach, Dooney & Bourke, Michael Kors, and other high-end brand names? Then do you need to be co-located and out on the same channels and out there in the same places with them, so they can easily compare and contrast your products with their products? Or are you setting yourself apart and are you going after a different market? Are you at a different level? Who are your competitors?

How do you set yourself up and how do you position yourself?

What is your geographic footprint? Are you going for brick and mortar at all? Is it going to be completely online to reduce costs? And are you online and brick and mortar? What kind of support are you going to need for online? Don't forget that online comes with website hosting and everything that you have to put in play. And what is that right mix that you need to find to target your target audience? All of these things are very important as you think through your vision so that you can identify who your target customer is and make sure that you are really identifying and thinking through that strategy for how you pick out your target customer out of everyone that is out there, that will resonate with your vision as opposed to someone else's vision, because those are the people that you need to be reaching.

Define Your Operations and Technology

Next is to define your operations and your technology. Websites are wonderful and require a strategy. What are you hoping to get out of your website strategy? Are you a service industry who needs a website for appearances and you're not going to attract and conduct business over the website? Many coaching and consulting businesses don't actually offer to pay over the website. They want to do negotiations and they have a website to feature the services, spark interests, and start the conversation, if you will, about their credibility, and the legitimacy of their business. But they want the flexibility of being able to negotiate rates with individuals at the time, and so they don't want to actually publish consulting or coaching services rates and program rates on the internet and to be able offer specials to give maybe longer rates for longest contracts, etcetera. There are different levels of security requirements for their websites than someone who is actually conducting high volume product sales through their website.

Define what your goals are for the website and that will inform your website strategy in terms of your social media presence, your cyber security strategy and the technology behind how it's hosted, whether it's blockchain or some other type, all of those other technologies that need to come into play for how you run your business and the investment that it will require in terms of the product, the coding behind your level of innovation. Those people who are high volume traffic and transaction processing require a high level of security if you're doing high volume of financial transaction processing or other things, you really need to have a blockchain strategy and or something even better. The Cloud is wonderful for small businesses who have a need for hosted applications and don't want to have an in-house data center, or a full IT staff. However, there again, you need to make sure that you have the proper security and pay for those investments to keep your data safe and secure and the transactions for your customers secure.

Operations and Technology Definition

You do not want to be making the news in that kind of a way for risking your customers' data in a data breach because you didn't take the time for risk management in thinking through your security and your operational integrity when you were setting up this business. So, thinking through all of those data security and integrity and infrastructure requirements is critically important at this point and the other thing is to look at scalability. Making sure that whatever you choose today is scalable and will fit over time because if you're not growing, you're contracting, and the whole vision that you have today may not be your vision two years from now, five years from now, ten years from now. You want to have some foresight and some planning and not be at maximum capacity the day that you open your doors, you don't want to go for a Fortune 50 kind of scale the day you open your doors either, because then that's just a wasted investment. However, you do need to look at something that has the capability to scale overtime as you grow, then the technology can grow with you and that you have the ability to scale into something that isn't so limited and that your growth is limited immediately upon startup

Define Your Core Strategic Model

and you cannot move forward due to the expense and time of changing technology systems.

Defining your organization and talent is a key element for many small businesses. Many, many entrepreneurs suffer from what we often call the "lone ranger" syndrome. In Chapter One, we discussed your DNA profile. The Technician profile loves to DO, if you have a Technician dominant DNA profile you may, from the moment you have the idea that you should be in business, that you have to wear every single hat in the business. So, you are the chief idea person, you are the chief accountant, you are the chief HR person, you are the chief marking person, you are the chief product person, you are the chief clerk, you are the chief fulfillment officer, you are the chief janitor, you are the chief check out person. It doesn't matter what role has to be done in that company, you wear every single hat and oftentimes, you get to a point where the business doesn't grow anymore, and they don't, they truly don't understand why. And it's that same thinking that got them started and maybe got them over some very rough times at the beginning, but then that keeps them from growing further because they have worn every hat.

From an IRS standpoint, there is another concern that may or may not come into play. If you have set your business up as a S Corporation, C Corporation or as an LLC, according to case law in all 50 US States and Commonwealths, you must keep regular meeting minutes of all decisions. When a small business suffers from the single person wearing all hats syndrome, often they forget to hold their accountability meetings. Before each decision is made is it documented and approved in the minutes? There is a list of about 100 items that the IRS will look at if you are selected for an audit. If you have not maintained that "corporate veil" by documenting all decisions and operating as a true legal business, corporation or entity, your business will be deemed for tax purposes a sole proprietorship and you will lose the tax benefits that come with the legal structure you have selected.

As a start up, you want to avoid, what we noted earlier, falling into the Fatal Assumption, understanding the technical expertise of the business, doesn't mean you understand all of the elements of running a technical business. Maybe it will start as ten minutes here, an hour there, two hours here because there will be a crisis or something went wrong, or they had an extra meeting or whatever. Then it becomes a pattern and it becomes the norm and then it's just the way things are being done. At that point, you've essentially bought a job, not a business and you lose the joy that came with that initial part of that business. You lose that energy and that passion that drove you to love that forty hours, that drove them to start that business and now they're caught up in doing the other work. It takes its toll on the other quadrants, you skip doctor and dentist appointments, you skip a walk, a work out, a healthy meal in favor of fast food. You skip a lunch with a friend, then a colleague, then miss a date night, maybe a school event for a child.

This is where the importance of the plan and the weekly accountability for the plan comes into play. At first, you take on some of those things. However, in your weekly or monthly or periodically, whatever that time period is for accountability, you ask "At what point can I afford to pay someone ten dollars an hour to do what they really love to organize this; to be an administrative person?" Or to do the books, or to be that bookkeeper?

You are providing a service to others. They went to school for it and they really enjoy doing that work and that skill. That's something they really like; You are improving the economy by hiring somebody, even if it's part time and giving them the opportunity to grow and do something that they really enjoy and now, You can get back to that core of why you started my business and focusing on what you love, your vision and having that plan in place so that everyone can be doing what they love and you can focus on growing your business instead of babysitting the functions that you don't like. You can have the right talent working on the right aspects of your business so that you can make sure that you have got the right job descriptions in place so that when you need someone, you can go get them, you can recruit them and you can find people with the right skills and you can pay them a competitive wage and you can understand what's needed.

This level of preparation is hard work, and yet it builds confidence. You have taken the actions you can take. You know that when the time is right that you are ready to have the conversation and bring the right person on board. You may meet them at a conference, an industry event or some other place. You have, in the words of the Thoreau quote, "passed an invisible boundary; new more universal liberal laws will establish themselves around and within me; or the old laws will be expanded, and interpreted in my favor in a more liberal sense, and I now live in with the license of a higher order of beings."

In an industry that has regulations or certifications or where there's training required, that you understand what that is and you have those materials ready to go and they're developed and you are not delayed in making sure that all those I's are dotted and T's are crossed. You not staying up late preparing materials, depleting energy and adding stress, which further depletes energy. When you are ready to go, you are confident and on top of it so you are focused on your vision and what's driving you. You bring that energy to every action you take, every client meeting, every email you send, the culture you create as you start this business and make it great. As you bring people in who are energized to play their role in also making your business great because they love what you and they do and they can play their role to the best of their ability and you build a team and you can lead that team towards implementing that vision and making this the best team and the best company that it can be to fulfill that vision.

Similar to organization and talent, defining your finance and accounting requirements is essential for sustainable success. Stating up with QuickBooks or some other similar product is often the right answer. But when is the right time to move to a bookkeeping service, a CPA, or some other solution? Having those milestones, having those checkpoints, is a key important area and there again. In the plan build in the interim goals and appropriate actions based on your understanding of the kind of business that you're in, the financial and accountancy requirements, any regulatory

Define Your Core Strategic Model

certification requirements, training requirements. Hold the accountability meetings and be realistic in measuring. This is key in understanding those milestones and working hand-in-hand with your tax and audit professional to set you on a path to understanding anything that is particular to your business, your vision, and making sure that you don't fall out of line with that. Regardless of the specific regulatory aspects, a general understanding the finances is important. It's unlikely that, unless you're a CPA and that is your core business, that it's going to be what you really wanted to get out of your vision. However, even if you hire a good and trustworthy CPA and/or bookkeeper, it is your business and you must master the fundamentals.

Likely, your vision is something not related to finance and accounting services unless that is the mission of your business, right? But understanding what is going on, what your financial position is, and enough to make sure that whatever decisions that you've made being able to adeptly read the financial report and the information that is coming out of those reports and interpret that will be critical in making valid decisions for your operations, for your organization, for your new customers, for your expansion, and in alignment with your vision as it wants to grow and expand; to look at it and say what do I take on? Is now the right time? When do I plan for that growth and expansion? How do I do that in a way that also respects the other core parts of my life vision so that I still have time to maintain my health and my relationships and my time and money freedoms so that I can have a full spectrum life of wealth and abundance and increase in every aspect of my life.

> "I'm constantly surprised how many people don't realize that if you're self-employed today, you're able to deduct 100 percent of the health-insurance premiums paid for yourself and your family."
>
> —**Mark Steber**

> "More than 5.4 million of the self-employed have absolutely no health insurance coverage, nor do 1.5 million of their children. In the end, we all pay for that..."
>
> —**Kit Bond**

You need to understand how you are doing and what strategies you can put in place so that you can make the appropriate decisions and make accountability and growth and iterative practice, and you can put in place the right accountability and understanding to manage that. You need to understand what the trigger points are to make the decision for when it's time to move from a base system to a larger system. How do you interview bookkeepers or accountants to make sure that they're taking care of my business and they have the needs of my business in mind? How am I making sure that you are getting the right reports, at the right level of detail, with the right frequency, and the right timing so that you can interpret them and make the business decisions to grow my business and keep it in alignment with that vision and the growth strategy and the plans that you have in mind. Those are the principles that you'll always have to maintain regardless of whether you keep it to yourself for you hire a staff, you outsource it, whatever strategy you maintain, you need to have that level of mastery and understanding of the reports, of what they're saying, and how to interpret them so that you understand that growth and you need to understand how to interpret that set of business statistics and reports and how they impact your company and the marketplace and where the trends are headed.

> "The self-employed person can't just go to the end of the year and say here's how much I owe. You are required by law to make payments during the year."
> —**Don Roberts**

Notes

CHAPTER 5
Define Your DNA Profile

"Remind thyself, in the darkest moments, that every failure is only a step toward success, every detection of what is false directs you toward what is true, every trial exhausts some tempting form of error, and every adversity will only hide, for a time, your path to peace and fulfillment."

—Og Mandino

Mastering Your Vision

IN THE FIRST four chapters, we have built a very strong blueprint of what your vision should be. For your life, and for your business. So now it's time to bridge from where you are today to where you want to be in that new vision for your business.

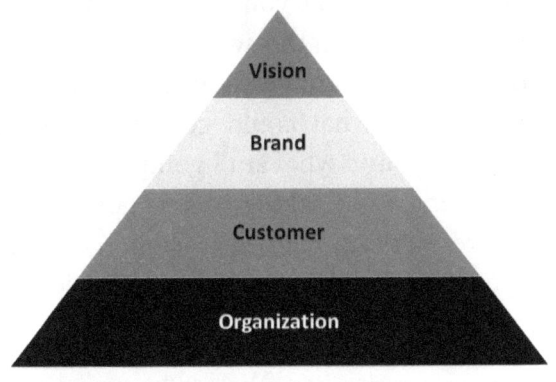

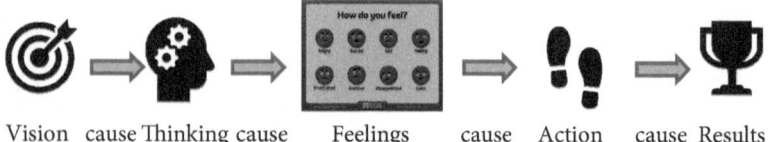

Vision cause Thinking cause Feelings cause Action cause Results

The key is to bridge from that blueprint that we've just built and looking into bridging into how to make that happen. So, the key is to master that vision. It's new, it's exciting, but it's kind of in its infancy. And like a brand-new child, whether it's a new infant that you just brought home from the hospital or a newly adopted child that you're welcoming into your family, you don't just bring it in and put it in its room and shut the door. No. You welcome it in, you feed it, you take care of it, and you bring it into the family and it takes a lot of attention and that's what this vision is going to take. And the more targeted and the more attention that you feed to it, the more successful that vision is going to be. And the more you master your thinking around that vision and focus your thoughts on that vision, then the more in control you are of the feelings that you have around it, right? By using the results formula in this way Your Vision causes you to Think correctly. You don't have time to generate limited Thoughts that create what could go wrong Feelings. The focused thoughts around what am I going to do, what action steps you are going to be taking, this is going to work out because you are working with the vision. You understand the vision, you add detail steps, clarity. It becomes part of who you are.

As you understand more about the products and the services, your target customer, you organization, your technology, finance and accounting this generates the expanded energy that pulls you forward in business and in life. There are myriad decisions and h.ow they're going to work together and how things are going to come together. Each week as you hold your accountability sessions, you can gain a picture of how circumstances, situations, competitive markets come into play and you take stock. Holding and refining the Vision and working the resulting formula leads to correct Thinking that, in turn creates the feelings that underscore the actions that I need to take and that ultimately create the success model.

All of those things work together to create that, and that becomes the curriculum of our life. We create, through our thinking, the feelings, which create our actions, which create our success. So, what are we going to do, what is that blueprint? How are we going to map that out? How are we going to source those things? How are we going to think through that? And that is from a mindset as we've talked about earlier of abundance and focusing on the fact that everything is created twice. First, it becomes an idea, then it comes into form.

Look around you, are you at your desk? The stapler, the computer, every single thing on your desk first became an idea, then it became a product that you then bought. It had to be created twice. And that is the principle that we're going follow here through creating your business. First, it's the thoughts, and now we're going about creating them into form through the actions that we're going to work through together and build this business into a success.

For purposes of this book, we'll define three different types of personalities that are at the core of your DNA profile.

- CEO—natural pioneer or entrepreneur that has ideas for new businesses, operates best at a summary level of detail, future thinking, craves change, multi-tasker and controls major decisions.
- Manager—efficient organizer, looks for patterns and themes, comfortable with the status quo, focused on the past, creates the processes, standardization.
- Technician—single-minded focus on the present and one task at a time, they are the doer, highly skilled at the product or service or the business.

In an ideal world we would all be 33.3% of each personality type and equally balanced. Very few of us are.

DNA Profile

CEO

Manager

Technician

Understanding your unique profile will help you develop the self-leadership skills to bring out the necessary roles create separation between you as the individual personality and you as the business leader.

> "Embrace the right values that may enable you achieve self-leadership & self-discipline and show commitment to these values unconditionally."
> **—Assegid Habtewold**

The next exercises may seem somewhat familiar. In Chapter 2 we looked at some of these topics from a business perspective. Here is where you take at look at your talents as a business owner. Are you more of a CEO, Manager, or Technical leader? What hat fits you most naturally and what other leadership styles will you need to either cultivate or find some other way as you company moves from start up to going concern? Introspection is the key here. No one else is looking at your answers.

Your Unique Purpose

What is your unique purpose? How does your why help you to make your business better? We just discussed that the pattern of thoughts become feelings become actions become success. Thinking through your trail of success, how does your why help you to make your business better? Take a few minutes, take some time and do this exercise. Take out a pen and write down from zero to ten. What are the things that I did between zero and ten that I really resonate with, that I remember, that were really important to me? What successes did I have? Did I climb to the top of the tree? Was I first to selected for that ball team? Did I win an award? Was I a spelling champion? Was I a leader on my sports team? What did I do? Was I the kindest person in the neighborhood? Did I make everybody feel their best or did I see whoever needed help and reached that helping hand? Was I the person who was the best friend? What was it that set me apart from my friends, my family, and the other kids in school? What was it? Or was it a hardship that I overcame?

Birth–10 Successes

Did I have a tough time growing up and I survived that? What is it that I am proud of, that made me a success between one and ten? Then, repeat that, between eleven and twenty. Do that same ten things, the exercise. Take another five minutes, just write down whatever comes to mind. Those same kinds of things. What are you proud of overcoming, what were you great at, what kind of trail of success, did you overcome abuse of some kind, a troubled relationship, heartbreak, did you get a scholarship, or did you make the sports team? What was it that set you apart?

11–20 Successes

And then, from twenty-one to your current age. What is it about you and your story that you overcame? Was it hard? Did you overcome addiction? Did you stop yourself from committing to suicide after a really hard problem? And now we're here to benefit from a new business that you're bringing about. Or have you always been a rock star, and you've gone from scholarship to top of your class to top of your executives.

21–Today Successes

Keeping a journal of these successes will help on days, hours when the Results Formula is not enough to turn around your thinking and you need to reframe your thoughts before you take actions on your business, relationships, health & wellness or time and money freedom. Meditation, rectangular breathing, listening to positive music are other methods to reconnect to your vision and energy source.

What is it about you that will make us connect to you and want to do business with you? What is important about your product or service? It is important for us to know these things. Write it down. And how, then take a step back. Take another five, ten minutes, and reflect. How do any of these strings of success, if at all, relate to the why in your vision? Does climbing that tree have anything at all to do with why you started a leather goods business? Maybe it doesn't. Or maybe it does. What is it that common thread that you can pick out to say what it is between these that have led you to this point? Because that's your story, that's your power, that's your ability to connect to the why and that will be powerful. Then, distill it down, and this is the hard part. This may take more like fifteen minutes to distill it down to two sentences. Because you only have thirty to sixty seconds to capture someone's attention. What can you say in thirty to sixty seconds to distill all that into a powerful statement about why and what your unique purpose is?

How You Do it Better

Now that you have the why, let's focus on the how. In chapter four, we talked about your business core strategic plan and we went through several different aspects of it: your products, your services, your IT, your HR, your finances, and your customers, all those aspects. We thought about your strategy from all those dimensions. You should have a really strong understanding at this point, of your blueprint and your strategy for how you're going to go to market. At this point, what is it, how do you do it better? What sets you apart as a business owner and leader? You understand that core strategic model should have that all right in front of you now. You've done this work. You know your CV, your resume, whatever you call it, and the history that sets you up for success in this business. If you don't have that at hand, put the book down, call it up on your computer, print it out or pull it up, whatever works for you and how you like to work, and have that at hand.

Now think about this, is it personal? Is it not just professional? Do you have a family or personal connection to this business that makes you more committed? Are you doing this because it's been in the family for years and years and years and you grew up with this inherited passion for it, or you came back to it? Maybe you pushed it away for a while and you just couldn't get it out of your blood. You did something else for a while and now you're back to it, or there's something about it because of something in your family, that just calls you and it's deeply personal. And that's part of that story that we uncovered in the last bullet point. Did you have a great mentor that really helped call this out in you and showed you this and revealed this talent? Or do you just have this great work ethic and this accelerated your results and you're just ready for this?

Why this is the right time

Do you have an entrepreneurial spirit or have a breakthrough idea or vision and your last company failed to see it and you couldn't get them to see it because of a bureaucracy or a process where they just couldn't get out of their own way, and so you're ready to take it on yourself because that's the way it needs to be. What is it? Pull all of that together and go through that same process. How do you do it differently? What sets you apart? Write it down. Make it long, make it messy. It's going to take some writing, it's not going to be pretty the first draft, it's going to be long, and it's going to be awkward because it comes from the heart. However, it's you, it's what you are called to do, right? And then keep working with it and get it down to that one, maybe two sentences, because it has to fit into that thirty to sixty seconds. One sentence, two sentences max. How you do it better? What is it about you? In all those documents, in your experience, in that family commitment, because of that mentor, because of this breakthrough idea.

How You Do it Better

Is it because of that strategic plan, because of the combination of all of it together? What is it that's how you do it better? Write it down, distill it down into a simple, powerful, one to two sentence statement.

Personal Mission Statement

Now it's time to write your mission statement. First, for sole proprietors, small business owners, this is not an exercise done by an executive committee at a corporation to hang over the door. Although I do recommend you hang it over the door. This is something that you commit to memory and you live by. This is something that, when you face an obstacle, you understand that an obstacle is a qualifier, that this is your go to say yeah, it's just a qualifier and this is my mission and my vision and this is why I'm doing this and this is why I'm getting through this, because this is an image that you want to have in your mind so that your mind clues to this and it replicates this mission statement out into the real world and in the truth of how your business is run. And people don't have to ask what your mission is. They can see that mission in how you treat them. So why are you doing this? What is your one sentence mission? The why you're in business? You should be able to do that by now with the work that we've done. This should be a five-minute exercise. Shouldn't take long. If you've been working with your vision, if you understand what your unique purpose is and why you've gotten into business and how you do it better, you should know. You should know what your mission statement is.

My Mission Statement

Value Statement

The next thing, what are your values? There shouldn't be many of these, three to five. They should be short, and you should incorporate them. If you have a small staff, you should say them before every meeting. If it's just you and start up mode or a couple of people, same thing. Say them on a regular basis. Have them sitting on your desk, read them every day, start the day with them. Here's an example: as certified life mastery consultants, we have five core values.

Define Your DNA Profile

1. We believe in people, we know that each one of us is far more powerful and can contain more potential than any circumstance, situation, or condition.
2. We believe in love and care. We bring sincere love and care to every interaction. We delight and surprise each other and our clients by anticipating wants and seeking to exceed expectations.
3. We believe in integrity. We live what we teach, we deliver what we promise.
4. We believe in fun, we create joy, laughter and fun in all aspects of our work.
5. We believe in growth. We grow by achieving our goals and exceeding our best.

Think about three to five things that you value, that you can incorporate into your daily routine very easily, that you want to inform your organization and you want to put in your training materials and your hiring materials and your recruitment strategy as your grow.

My Core Values
1.
2.
3.
4.
5.

You want to be a part of the culture and how you do business and you want people to understand that that is who you are. You will want them to know what you stand for because you've incorporated them into your actions and how you work every day. People can see whether you like to have fun or not, people can see whether you operate from integrity, people can see whether you believe in them, people can see whether you love and care for them, and people can see whether you believe in their growth or not. Those are easy. See what matters to you and your organization and put those into place.

It's important; it's a major differentiator when you don't have values that are long or convoluted or merely aspirational and not embedded in how you work every single day. It's a key differentiator and many studies, I'm not going to cite them all here or in this book, but I can tell that is one of the differentiators between good and great, when you live the values that you state and you incorporate them into your daily work.

Your DNA Profile

So now, comes the important part. You've got your story, tell it. Work with marketing, who understands your unique purpose, how you do it better, what your mission statement is, what your values are. Build those relationships with your target customers. Right now, there are hundreds of cancer charities with similar missions. But people choose to give to the one that is most resonant with them. That's why we keep starting more instead of only giving to the American

Cancer Society. They may be the first and the best known, but it doesn't resonate with everyone. And if there's only the need for one, other ones wouldn't start. Tell that story, and work with someone who can help you tell that story affectively, in the right channels where your target customers are. Don't just blindly go out over social media, any target, any random channel in social media, telling your story. Do it in a controlled, strategic way with a marketing plan. It's important to plan it out and coordinate each of the different messages. There are different types of target customers.

They're in different places in their journey. You'll tell the same core elements of the story but you'll switch it up. You may have a more sophisticated story over here, someone else's in a different point in their journey, and you'll vary it a little bit. Not to the point where you're changing integrity, but if you have a twenty-year old work history, you'll tell the companies that you worked for, or the stories about the customers that you had or the works that you did, based on what they told you about their life. First you listen to them, you find out what's important to them first if you're having a discussion with them in a social session and you're getting to know them one on one. Or you're meeting them on social media and you're trying to create a relationship with them and you're finding out who they are and you're building a relationship with them through social media and you're gaining followers, you find out who responds to you and you don't necessarily offer a blanket response to everybody. You look at who's responding and you respond in kind.

You target your customers by how they respond to you and what they are interested in. Going back to the leather goods store, if you've got products for men and for women, you respond differently to the men than to the women. It's not rocket science, it's not a lack of integrity, it's understanding that men are interested in different products than women are. What you have to do is understand your market, understand your product, understand your mission, and tailor your story and build that relationship. If you're going to be an independent business person, you have to build a relationship with your customers. It's unlikely that you're going to succeed the Wal-Mart way and build up enough volume to succeed. You're going for sustained relationships over time. You're going to want them to buy that first item and fall in love with it and want to come back and say okay the next time I need x.

I'm going to come back and look here for this kind of item or product again, or service again, because I found what I wanted, they took good care of me customer service wise, whatever it was, because of the relationship that I formed, right? So, that's your target, that's how you build customers through heart-centered marketing in this economy and understanding your story, your customers, your unique purpose, how you do it better, that's what separates you from every other business that's out there vying for attention in this mass market and in this whirlwind that we all compete in for attention and business every day.

You now have your core DNA profile. This is much more that just your brand story. You will have recognized many of the same elements from the Brand Story chapter. However, this is personal and as we know from science, no one has the same DNA. Even in the same family, no one has the same genetic makeup and not everyone in the same family has the same life experiences. You may choose to use elements of your DNA profile in your Branding or not. How most successful small business owners use this most effectively is in developing the mental faculty of Will.

Will is not will power as we have come to think about in in maintaining a diet or other change, it is the pull energy that drives us, expands our Vision and reminds us of the Why, and our purpose.

> "The will to win, the desire to succeed, the urge to reach your full potential . . . these are the keys that will unlock the door to personal excellence."
>
> **—Confucious**

Notes

CHAPTER 6

Unlocking The Code For Success

> "A business absolutely devoted to service will only have one worry about profits. They will be embarrassingly large."
>
> —**Henry Ford**

Keep Going and Growing

At this point, we're into building and the key thing for building and understanding is to source. How do we source? We take a look at activities that we can do each day to source for, to know what activities will move us forward. I'll look for our long-term activities. We can look for short-term activities too, so those are activities that I can do. What can I do in five minutes that'll move me forward? What can I do in thirty minutes that'll move me forward? What activities can I do in one day that'll move me forward? This, then, helps to create short and long action plans and helps us when we tend to get stuck. Of that brainstorming list, what of those ideas give me electricity and energy, what feel constricting? I prioritize the ideas that feel energizing and expansive and deprioritize the ones that feel constrictive.

Here's an example. They'll have days where we need structure and we need direction. We have this great vision and we live in this whirlwind of constant activity right? We've got the garbage that needs to be taken out, and the dishes that need to be washed, and maybe we have kids that need to be cared for and we have a primary relationship that needs caring and we have family or extended family and we have friends and social life and all of these things and demands for our time right? So that's our whirlwind of things that we need to maintain, and we have to go to the cleaners and the laundry and so we can't go outside looking like a mess if we're going to try and run a business right? We have all of that that we have to go and we look and we say, how are we going to do this? We have to manage our conditions, our circumstances. One of the key things that we can do first is put in place a structure. Using your calendar is one of them. Looking forward into your calendar the night before, or the week before, or both, using the thought process of how I do I forecast, how do I manage my calendar to plan out recurring items and keep important actions that will drive my vision forward?

How do I make sure I prioritize getting those things on that calendar? I previously shared the story of a professor who gave his class a set of ping pong balls, some small pebbles, some sand and some water and a jar and said fill it all up with no additional direction. Those that started with the ping-pong balls then put in the rocks then sand and finished with the water accomplished the task. Because they started with the biggest item first or the highest priority first and then the smaller things worked their ways around the ping-pong balls and filled up some available space and the sand filled up available space and then the water filled up the rest of the available space. But if you did the exercise in reverse, there was no room for the big things. So if you started with the water, or the sand, and you filled it up, there was no room for the ping-pong balls or the highest priority and you filled up your day with emails and the trivia and the laundry and the washing the dishes and the big things like starting the business and getting the goals and those things never came to pass. So, we put in place structure and that calendar and that prioritization.

Calendar for the month of _____

Sunday	Monday	Tuesday	Wednesday	Thursday	Friday	Saturday

Then, we source the ideas and we understand what the actions that I can be taking are. The what can I do in five minutes, fifteen minutes, thirty minutes, a day? So now, you have your ping-pong ball, your rocks, your sand, and your water, right? What are some of these things that I can do that need to be done to move my business forward? And I prioritize them and I ask again, what needs to be done? And I schedule those in and I give myself a little bit of a pass. Things are going to come along, right? And I may have to reschedule. But I only reschedule once without taking a really hard look and asking how bad do I really want this? If I'm moving something constantly, it's because I really don't want to do this or because I don't understand why it needs to be done or somebody should be doing this for me. I need to be delegating this to somebody who understands this better. What is the issue? Do I need to break it down into something?

Maybe that one-day task is too big. Maybe it needs to be broken down into smaller segments. What is up with that task right that's holding me back from accomplishing it? And then, I arrange it in the calendar and I—I hold that calendar as priority and that structure. And I do that not only with that business, but as we've talked about throughout this book, I do that with the other priorities within the other aspects of my business or in my life. And if I really value and I have some big goals, in areas of my health, on my relationships, or time and money freedom, whatever that is, I make sure I prioritize that on my calendar as well. And then, I fill in those other smaller blocks of time and I figure out how to do that so then I'm sure.

Refreshing your services and products.

In addition to your periodic accountability meetings with your personal accountability, each of the aspects of your strategic vision needs that same level of accountability. Meeting with whoever is in charge of each area of these strategic components of your business on a periodic basis is key, going through each of the reports. Is it a meeting with yourself and exercising self-leadership, self-management, and accountability? Or is it working as a team leader? Does it matter? The key is the accountability and the understanding of managing reports, understanding what the reports are telling you about your services, about your products and the performance of how they're doing in the market place. You've got a suite of products and you've got a history over time and you can watch and see how that performance is.

You may be in love with a particular product, but its sales are lagging over all the other ones. It may be time for you to take a hard look at that product and say just because I am in love with this product, doesn't mean my target customers are or the market place is. What do I do about that? Have I correctly targeted the right customers? Do I do a survey? Do I need to refresh this product? Source the correct action and you'll bridge the gap between performance and the target. What is it that's not appealing? Or have I done the surveys and I need to go in and read some of the open comments and find out, and do some product adjustments based on the feedback. and I'm just not paying attention. and the customers are voting with their dollars because I love this product and I've been reluctant to take the data that's been coming in on these surveys and not make the changes that my customers are telling me about because I personally love this product, even though my customers are telling me no. Where am I at? Taking and putting myself above the circumstances and the situations and notice what I'm noticing about my business, about my products, about my services and seeing where we're at and running it like a true leader and making those hard decisions. Seeing what has to be done or are they begging for something new? In those same surveys or other things, other social media, are they liking what they're seeing or are they saying "Hey, I love this this and this but I would also love a coordinating x, I want to add this, and you're not selling me this. Can you add this product to the line? Can you add this to the line?"

When analyzing the survey results, then it is important to put on the independent analyst hat and rise above the results and detach from them personally to be able to take the stance in the face of constructive feedback: I may have become comfortable with my suite of products, and I'm not challenging myself to grow or to expand to look for new wholesalers, or new suppliers to grow and to expand because I've gotten comfortable. What is it that I need to be doing, to look to grow and what's going on?

Or is it a quality issue. Maybe I need a new vendor, I've had a lot of returns, some off quality, or maybe I've had trouble shipping on a certain product and it's not related to the product at all, it's related to the time of delivery and the product is just fine, but they're using a different delivery service than they were before and instead of taking two days, it's taking four days to get there, and people are impatient and they really want your product and they're not willing to wait four days. Getting to the root cause of what's going on and making the appropriate changes, that's what's important and doing that on a regular basis is critical. I recommend weekly, biweekly at most, and refreshing that plan, understanding what it's going to take. It takes lead time to make those changes, implement those changes, and see the results over time.

Refreshing, Reviewing Your Target Customers

Who and where are your target customers? For a new business, look at your initial marketing plan. How is that working out? Are you targeting them correctly? Are you reaching them? What are your initial results. Do you need to change that? Are things changing over time? Are you attracting new customers in different demographic groups to constantly refresh your customer base or are your customers aging with you? Is that the sign of a contracting business? What's going on with your business? This one is probably a lengthier review that you want to conduct on a monthly or quarterly basis. Because you won't see necessarily unless you're in a very innovative, trend-setting business where markets change at the drop of a hat, then you'd want to adjust the frequency to much more frequently than the typical business. But if you're in a typical business, you'd probably want to do this on a monthly or quarterly basis.

Look at how are things trending over a period of time and a longer period of time. How are things happening? How are buying patterns changing? Are cultural norms changing? Are there new products coming in and disrupting the market and affecting buying patterns and lead times? What's going on in the marketplace? And then adjust your review based on your findings and your competitive analysis. It's important that you keep your finger on the pulse of your own business in this area but also on the competitive marketplace because you want to stay relevant and the marketplace changes. It's a very dynamic time that we're living in. Many new businesses are forming, a lot of great new visions, new ideas, new thoughts, new products, and new exciting times and with that comes disruption, change, and the exciting part about this, is that opportunity. So, conditions and situations are qualifiers. How do you want it?

How bad do you want it? How much do you want to grow? How exciting is this to you? And, how much does it feed you and pull you in to wanting to grow and finding these customers and reaching these customers with your vision and who you can reach and what you can touch, whose lives you can impact and what changes can you make by offering this product, this service. And what you can do with your work in the world? How cool is this? How important is this to you? That will draw and determine how often you do this, how much you refresh this, how you grow, how you expand you vision, and how often you do this work and what energy and excitement and vitality you bring to this work. If you approach it as a routine task that needs to be done, it comes with a completely different energy and thought process and mindset than if you bring to it "Oh my gosh who do I get to serve today, what excitement, what new value, who can I touch today, whose life can I impact today?" And when you bring that mindset, that excitement, that energy, to serving this and looking at those reports, and working with whoever your lead for customer service is, then that energy and that innovation sparks growth and innovation and excitement is realized.

Refresh Your Operation and Technology

Now we're onto refreshing your operations. So, looking at your technology footprint and security to ensure capacity, security, and matching whatever new innovation, new ideas, growth, and advancements, and the new innovations in the external market place, etcetera, is vital. Things are changing really rapidly. For the longest time, Facebook was the place to be for small businesses. People built entire empires, followings, curated businesses and careers based on Facebook and its various iterations around this. And with the new changes in Facebook, those businesses are going away. Doesn't make sense for your business. Who are your target customers? How do they get their information now? Are your target customers still on Facebook given the sensitivities about information and how it's consumed over the last few months? Or have they switched to LinkedIn or some other media for getting their information? Or are they still there because they have no other creative outlet? Think about it, talk with other people in the area, look and see what your competitors are doing.

Think about your target strategy. Where do you need to be to find your customer audience, to craft your message? There are some other opportunities for technology, getting your message out there. How do you stay forward with that? How do you make sure that your applications are secure, everything is backed up, and you're ready for everything? Working with your IT person, if you're not an IT literate or advocate kind of person, sometimes you can go in like we talked about in the last bullet point, with a routine attitude or mindset. Here, again, it's critical. Find somebody who knows this, that this is their passion, who loves staying abreast of what's new, what's innovative and has the capability to talk with you in a way that makes you not only understand what they're talking about but excited for the capability of what it can do to move your business forward. It's critical that you understand the technology, the movement, the progress, and how it can impact your business in a way that gives you the reach and the power, the stability and the security that it needs, particularly if you're processing transactions over the internet. If you're using it as a marketing and a web presence tool, the security aspect isn't as important, but getting your message out is critical.

You'll have a different strategy than somebody who is processing transactions. Make sure that whoever you're working with really is in lockstep and alignment in understanding with the right technology, and the right fit for your strategic model, where you're headed and the fit for your business, your vision, and is keeping you current, safe, and scalable for where you're headed.

Refresh Your Organization and Talent

Your organization and talent are the heart and soul of the business. We talked a good bit earlier about how the lone ranger syndrome can sometimes affect small businesses and here's where you want to keep your finger on the pulse and use self-leadership, self-management, and that mindset of what would I love and how does my business vision fit into my life vision for passing that test for when it's time to let loose the lone ranger vision and sole proprietor vision and bring in either 1099 contractors, outsource to a bookkeeper for finances, or maybe outsource payroll to a payroll organization or an agency who does those kinds of things to keep you out of those kinds of time management kinds of activities that can worry you about all of the various benefits and regulations and certifications and things like that to make sure that you're withholding everything accurately and getting everything correct as you expand. Look at making sure that you have a team.

Some people really miss being part of a corporate culture and they naturally want to lead a team and so they're not subject to the lone ranger syndrome. But they've got other challenges, so how do they put in place the documentation and the consistency in building that culture of training materials and processes and things and not just starting a handbook or starting this or starting that and never getting it rolled out and putting in place all of those things. How can you get those things not just started, but completed so that you've got consistency and putting all of that in place for your small business so everyone understands and there's an understanding of fairness across different areas of your business. And you're working together as you grow and everyone has that common understanding of what the company is, and what the values are, and what's important and how you're going to work together and grow as a team as a culture.

It's really important to put those things, the plans and those materials and those spots and those benefits together intentionally, and there are all kinds of resources out there that you can leverage and work together to find and outsource to and to make your life so much easier as you look, grow and develop that mindset so that you can leverage all kinds of materials that you can replicate and onboard that talent and expand those benefit programs and accommodate your expanded workforce so that everyone is included and understands what makes your business great, what makes it unique, and how to treat your customers. Because if you treat your customers right and you treat your employees right, your employees from top to bottom will make your customers happy and they will continue to keep coming back and your business will continue to keep growing.

Refresh Your Finance and Accounting

Finally, in the area of structure and accountability and growing a business, it's reviewing and growing your finances and accounting. What are the breakpoints between doing it yourself, adding staff, and outsourcing? Understanding, there again, bookkeeping, QuickBooks, CPA, a system. When do you actually need to go to an ERP system, or clue system? Understanding what those breakpoints are, when do you hire an accountant? At what point and at what skill level, every business is different and that's why so many businesses hire a business coach or someone with objective outside expertise to help them determine what the breakpoint is for them. Because each person comes with a different skill set, a different business model, a different strategic model, a different set of competitive demands and family capabilities and life vision right? So setting up that weekly accountability, where am I at? What was my budget going in, what do I have left between my start up budget and my carry over business?

How quickly am I getting up to speed, how am I staying on track with meeting my targets, financial goals? Where am I at, how quickly am I expanding? What are my expansion goals, am I meeting all of those targets? Am I expanding quicker? What are my market disruptions? All of these things are relevant. What is my capability for reading a financial report, understanding it, applying it, and making those decisions appropriately and what is my access to a CPA and great accounting? Do I have a background in finances and accounting and I just do an online tax program or do I have a really complex global model where it's an online business and I sell around the world and I am open 24/7 and I have multiple currencies. That's a far different answer than I have a small service business and I have five customers in my local town in one currency. So, each person has to make that decision for themselves. It has, in no way, shape or form, a one size fits all answer. Consequently that's where you set up that weekly and or periodic financial reporting and accountability checkpoint for self-leadership.

How am I doing, am I understanding this, am I understanding what people are telling me, do I understand all of this? And what do I have to put in place? What are the geographic limitations in my business? What licensing do I have to put in place? What sort of regulations and compliance are unique to my business? And all of that as I think through the complexities of each business as I advise. I don't think I've ever given the same answer twice to any business I've ever worked with. True, that sets me apart because I treat each client that I work with as an individual. But I think that's the fundamental premise that each of you should work with. What is your vision? What is your capability? What is your life circumstance? And how do I fit this business into my life and make the appropriate decisions that are right for me and my business? What makes sense to me and act accordingly.

And what can I do to make my life and my vision make sense so that I'll continue to love it, be passionate about it, and want to continue to grow it and not get tired of it. And want to serve this vision, this mission, and keep it growing and keep it going, and continue to make this vital and strong and continue to unlock the code for my success story.

> "Intuition is a wisdom of formed by feeling and instinct—a gift of knowing without reasoning ... Belief is ignited by hope and supported by facts and evidence—it builds alignment and creates confidence. Belief is what sets energy in motion and creates the success that breeds more success."
>
> **—Angela Ahrendts**

www.ingramcontent.com/pod-product-compliance
Lightning Source LLC
Chambersburg PA
CBHW020456220526
45464CB00002B/1004